Where do we go from here?

By Kenneth Kuntz

Pray for Fr John Murry of Nantucket that he will be forgiven for his transgressions.

"The only regret I have is not doing all that I wanted to do in life."- Alfred Kuntz

A thank you to all the researchers that made this book possible.

IT'S SO QUEER

Katahdin seemed to be eluding me. Maine's highest mountain found a way for years to conceal itself. Whether with fog, trees or blowing snow, I wasn't able to see any sight of it for some 20 years.

Lou-deane was a gorgeous red-head that I met by chance on a ferry, far from the backwoods of Maine. It came to be that she invited me to the north woods of Maine. She was going to visit her parents grave, and promised that I would see moose. I was accepting of her offer, not just to see the moose, as much as to spend time with a woman I was instinctively and completely attracted to.

Our travel passed through her hometown, and she pointed out the one room schoolhouse that she used to ride her horse to when she attended it. She pointed out several moose on the way which was a thrill for me, as I had never seen them before. I found it amusing that she would say "there's a moose!" when their size made it impossible to miss them. Tall, majestic, and unique, their sighting was just a prelude of the magical week I was to spend appreciating all that nature could deliver.

I had spent much time alone in the swamps and along the shore of the great South Bay observing nature, a pastime instilled in me by my father. New York's Long Island presented a child with a variety of life to discover. Muskrats, birds, snakes and fish of all kinds fascinated my boyhood. I could look for them for hours, then spend hours more watching them go about their business. Wildlife shows we are creatures of habit. People watching became another form of life to witness, and at an early age, the most difficult. I still see in young children's eyes the confusion and fascination of dealing with their parents or friends, or even strangers. For me, confusion and fear were the headlines of the newspapers, with crime family murders happening on almost a daily basis. I would be outside as a child and air raid sirens would be going off as the start of a drill to take shelter from a nuclear attack by the Russians during the cold war. What are these people about?

As Lou-deane and I checked into the lakeside cabin that would be our residence for the next two weeks, the thoughts and fears of my childhood activity were far from my mind. Presenting to me a nature lover's dream, she had rented a deep-woods retreat that would be a well-remembered adventure, no doubt, for all time.

She stood at a height that was perfect for kisses. She received them well, and kiss we did upon entering the rustic dwelling. It wasn't an out of control, passionate, I don't even care what I'm doing kind of kiss; but it was a tender and long, non-wandering hands type of kiss…for we both knew we had the time ahead for much more.

We did fill those weeks with caressing and kissing, clutching and cuddling, massage and coddling. Things we have all done that make us stare into space, as we go about the acts that nature instilled to culminate in propagation. In our prime age to experience nature's desire, actions came without thought. So fluidly that among the pine trees and on the crystal clear lakes, we partook in natural actions that would fill a romantic novel.

Perhaps it was those feelings that made it so hard to understand homosexuals. So far from my thoughts would be for me to engage in sexual activity with another male. I found that the thought of two males engaging in intimacy on any level, gave me the same feeling I got when I watched a film showing a cheetah taking down a gazelle. A sick/gut-wrenching/disgusting feeling. Understandable was when the United States passed the Defense of Marriage Act. It kept marriage as a union between a man and a woman. I felt that this bond between male and female should be preserved as such. I didn't even think it was necessary because marriage was always defined as between a man and a woman. Since before recorded history, this union of male and female was held by society as a monumental event. Marriage was supposed to be a once in a lifetime experience. It brought man and woman together so they could enjoy their differences and to that end, create a family. Religions make it a sacrament or other holy and blessed state. I knew I wasn't alone in my feelings. For years I have asked people their feelings on gay marriage and gays in general, and overwhelmingly, I heard objections. I would ask people from all over the world and of both sexes.

It is now February of 2015 as I write and today, for the first time, I looked up marriage in the classical dictionaries and found the definition had changed to include "opposite sex and same sex", the same sex being a relationship like that of a traditional marriage. There is no way that the two relationships are the same on a realistic observation. The gay proponents feel that they are just the same as straight couples. How can that be? They are two of one sex and tradition has the definition of opposite sexes. If it were the same thing they would be able to have sexual relationships like traditional marriages. Without getting into a graphic description, let me just say that males are not physically the same as females so to have a traditional relationship is physically impossible.

It is the singularity of marriage that should be at the core of the marriage question. To change the meaning, to add other forms of so-called marriage, would be to change a basic building block of society, a cornerstone of the nuclear family that sociologists say is necessary for optimal human development. As well spoken as many of the proponents of the "gay marriage" argument are, no matter how well composed their words are to support their cause, passage of a gay marriage law leaves our most important life long societal union, that of the union of a man and woman, without a name. There would be no word that specifically designates this union that has been around since before recorded history. How arrogant we are in this day and age to feel we know better than our ancestors to rearrange relationships, society and human interaction. I am not a bible thumper, but I had to look to see what the bible had to say about homosexuality. The bible is of course the basic beginning of written laws that governs so much of the world. Do not kill, do not steal, and other statements of universal and timeless standards of right and wrong are written.

I was surprised to see how clearly the verses in the bible rejected homosexuality, and how severe the penalties. It was certainly a concern 3421 years ago when it was forbidden in the bible. Also when I looked into other religions, I found that homosexuality is shunned in every major religion. I can say after research that world wide, on a religious level, that anyone who claims to follow a faith or set of religious doctrine is going against their religion if they support homosexuality. It is spoken against in doctrines of all religions.

I was always with the feeling that consenting adults can do what they want. But I can say I don't think that it has to be broadcast to the general public which lately has become commonplace. I don't see the need to announce to the world that I am straight. Ok…everybody…I want you all to know that I am straight. I have been this way since a young age and I feel a load off my shoulders to tell you now. Do you care? Is it necessary? I would feel just fine if everyone was to keep their personal life personal. I would only expect to hear about personal relationships from a close friend, or if I went searching for the information. It's like everyone has lost respect for eachother. My friend Bob sums it up by the simple statement of "I don't care what two guys do together, I just don't want to see them kissing on my TV".

We now have it where children in California can use any bathroom depending on their gender preference that day. Even for those who agreed that this would be a good idea, I have to relate the story of a young girl who was assaulted by a male. Her parents say they couldn't get her to go to school for months after that . Now with the "new bathroom law" they fear she will flip out if a boy walks into the girls bathroom. Doesn't that young girl deserve the privacy that was part of common sense rules in the past? Why should society entertain rules that disrupt normal social order? Should the majority of children that are developing traditional, healthy normal lives be exposed to confusing and frankly dangerous laws? It's no stretch of the imagination that mixing the sexes causes problems.

The best intentioned laws run astray. Mao Zedong, the Chinese leader, instructed the Four Pest campaign between 1958 and 1962. The idea was to have the people of China exterminate mosquitoes, rats, flies and sparrows. They were considered as threats to the people, especially the sparrow- as the sparrow would eat grain that was in short supply and it was a food for the people. This did not, however, end in the desired results. By 1960, scientists believed that sparrows had normally eaten a lot of insects and without the sparrows the insects multiplied, reducing rice yields, and exacerbated the great Chinese famine in which 20 million lives were lost. The North American Free Trade Agreement opened the door to foreign manufacturing to supposedly benefit everyone, but now we (the US) not only are a nation without jobs, we are a nation without factories. History is full of government actions that had the best intent, but ended in disaster. Why would we want to change laws, principles and customs that have been around forever just to entertain those who want to pretend they are like married people? They shouldn't be allowed to invent weddings where there are two grooms, or two brides, or when one of the two women dresses up in a man's clothes and the other is dressed as a bride. How are two women going to fulfill the classic vow to procreate? Gay adoption isn't procreation, it is again an attempt to imitate the traditional nuclear family.

The human mind has such an ability to expand thoughts about anything. We can look at sociological studies that define human behavior. A thought planted in someone's head when they are young can develop to specific behavior when they mature. Sometimes it takes less time. Once I was looking for a movie to watch with a friend. I went to the video tape rental store (the way it was then). I looked at a movie called Natural Born Killers. On the cover it had the names of Rodney Dangerfield and Woody Harrelson, who were comedians to my knowledge. So I thought we would enjoy a good comedy together. The movie turned out to be a supposed satire about two characters that go out and just start killing people- not funny at all. Quite appalling actually. The reason I bring the movie up is that some young people who saw the movie committed terrible crimes of murder after seeing the movie. Some thirteen different murder scenes were attributed to the fact that the criminals were influenced by the movie and no one knows the true number. This isn't the only film attributed to motivating people to commit the most horrible crimes imaginable. Look up Ariel Castro if you really want to be sick. He was motivated by pornographic films. My point is that contemporary media is swamping us with homosexual support and attempting to convince everyone that we should be loving and caring and accepting of the lifestyle…to everyone, to everything. Just the exposure alone is going to compel the young to experiment. The planting of a seed of thought is going to lead children to experiment, because what child doesn't experiment? That is how we develop. What are the ramifications of the young being exposed to what used to be considered adult topics. Isn't youth tumultuous enough without people questioning what gender they are? Now kids are exposed to the need to think about what gender they are. Aren't parents stressed enough without society forcing acceptance of nontraditional, unconventional lifestyles on their children?

Certainly as a nation, we promote it too. In the Sochi Olympics, the hosting Russians asked other nations to not make a big thing about homosexuality. Their reasoning was that they didn't want their young to be exposed to it. What does the US do? We send over gay people who were past Olympic Champions to represent us. What happened to being respectful of others' wishes? Why can't we respect those who are against promoting it? Why do we (and other nations) feel we have to bring sexual preferences into the Olympics at all? The same with international policies. US financial aid to some nations goes with an understanding that the receiving nation must provide better conditions for homosexuals. National leaders in poor nations state that they do not believe their morals should be held at ransom for them to receive the much needed aid. They have their own desire to bring their children up as they see fit.

The classical, conventional and customary way to raise children is in a male/female household. Do those who feel that exposing children to a house that has parents of the same sex is think it's going to be healthy? With statistics saying there are around 3% of people that are are not straight, the chances are that a child adopted by gays is going to be straight. What is the result of that interaction going to be? Is the child going to have some conflict in their thoughts or life? For me, this is the most valid reason I have against the homosexual promotion. Why are we priming our kids to question thoughts of basic traditional lifestyles? We are confusing the masses to please and legitimize the few. One observation of the homosexual attempt to be like everyone else is that they are constantly coming up with a new way to describe themselves. Gay became lesbian-gay, then LGB, the LGBT, and now I understand it's LGBTQ. A nurse I know was taking a course on sexual assault forensic evidence collection and had a whole day of instruction devoted to sexual assault of an LGBTQ victim. The instructor explained that Q stands for queer. The nurse said she was wondering, aren't they all queer? She was of course referring to the traditional definition of queer…strange, odd, peculiar. It was considered a label of homosexuals as I grew up, and now homosexuals have apparently reappropriated the word to mean a group that is of non-heterosexual identities. Go figure. So much is being created in the queer groups that my friend read an article in trying to keep abreast of the topic and came to the conclusion that she had no idea what they were talking about. Just now as I was looking up words I read in an article, such as "cisgender", the Merriam Webster dictionary, at the time, could not come up with a definition. Then there is the word homophobic. To me, a phobia was a fear of something. Medically, it is still "an overwhelming, exaggerated, irrational and often disabling fear". Mainstream queers define homophobic as hate towards them. Queers have called me homophobic, but I could tell them that I wasn't afraid of them…..and I don't hate them. Now it seems all of society has accepted that homophobics are discriminatory towards gays or have irrational dislike. Word meanings are changed. Well that covers a lot of territory. It seems to fall into a generic "you are with us or against us' ' philosophy. If you don't support us, then you are a hateful, bigoted, mean person. It seems that homosexuals can come up with a zillion ways of looking at sex, but you are wrong if you don't agree with them. You are then an enemy and there is no in between. I personally feel it's wrong and I don't want to have you twist things around to have me think differently...or represent me differently than I am. I feel it is unhealthy both physically and mentally. At times, the reasoning that gays give gets so convoluted that I don't know what to think. They can change the meaning of the word phobia, of the word queer, but they cannot change the meaning of marriage. Things are too confusing now, not only for homosexuals, but for straight people too. Of the hundreds of times I have asked people of their views on homosexuality, the response that summed it up for most is what my friend Pauline said. "I don't care what anyone does, just don't yell at me." Most people would just rather go on without concerns for what is influencing the world as long as no one causes any problems for them. I guess it's natural for people to care for their own isolated existence than to expose themselves to the criticism of standing up for their true feelings. However, on this topic I was surprised to see people's facial expressions change to a serious, concerned look. When asked about homosex and marriage, people in general had a negative commentary. The simplest reaction was from a 30 something Russian female immigrant who said "it's just wrong." With all that we have to say about immigrants, at least they have morals. With all the interviews I have done, it seemed that the only true supporters of the homosexual lifestyle were gays themselves, and those people who think it's ok for individuals to do whatever they please, including drugs, committing suicide, etc. Add to that how comments on writings and articles about gays on the internet are extreamly anti gay. Some people were violently against gays. Of course so many people in our society are so stressed out to just put food on the table, take care of the kids, or just get through the day so they don't take any other opinion on a topic than what is the mainstream, right, socially acceptable, least confronting view.

Are children indoctrinated to the gay cause without consent of their parents? One parent was mad because he and his child were watching the Rose Bowl parade and two gay guys were getting married on a float. The parent said how am I going to explain this to my son? And he should be upset. Any seed of thought about such mature subjects should be introduced by a parent and he certainly projected those thoughts. The amount of pro-homosex information given to us is so overwhelming that once I went to search out the bible verses on a Christian website and the fact that I was searching for "homosexual" in bible verses made ads come on the site that advertised gay cruises, gay dating, and gay this and that. Imagine, a mainstream Christian website that had advertising that artificial intelligence pre-programmed promoting homosexuality. That's not intelligent at all. It's out of control. Certainly like so many other things it is for money that they promote homosexuality in this way. The shock value makes the young and curious watch programs with homosexuals and promoters know that. Homosexual talk show hosts boast that their jokes are never about stereotypes of men and women as if stereotypes are not a reality. Those with power and money use media personalities to promote their own beliefs and legitimize them. What politician doesn't support a cause to get votes and financial support. Vast amounts of money were spent to establish the present status of gay marriage in some states. This is culminating in the fact that states that have definitions of marriage being between a man and a woman are being told by federal judges that they can't do that. It is announced that this state and that state are the newest to allow same sex marriage, but in reality, they are the newest states to be forced to marry same sex couples. I always thought we were a nation where majority rules and I couldn't for the life of me understand how we as a nation were getting laws of same sex marriage passed while so many opposed the idea. It turns out that "majority rules" was the basis of our nation looking more closely at the rights of the minority. The founders believed in the natural rights theory, which holds that the rights come from nature or from God and can not be taken away without consent. Therefore, the majority has no legitimate power to vote away or otherwise abridge the natural rights of political, ethnic, religious, or other minorities. The founders had great respect for the will of the majority, but also understood that, as James Madison said at the Virginia Constitutional Convention, "In republics, the great danger is, the majority may not respect the rights of the minority." Thomas Jefferson in his first inaugural address said, "All, too, will bear in mind this sacred principle that though the will of the majority is in all cases to prevail, that will, to be rightful, must be reasonable, the minority possess their equal rights, which equal laws must protect and to violate which could be an oppression.

Gay marriage is not a right given by God. Doctrine of biblical basis clearly states that marriage is between a man and a woman. With the right for gays to be married denied by God, according to natural rights theory, the only way for gays to be given the ok to marry would be because it is natural. It's a stretch for me to see that same sex unions all of a sudden became a natural thing in the last few years. U.S. District Judge Shelby talks of the "Right to form a family" that is strengthened by a partnership based on love, intimacy and shared responsibilities." The right to form a family is denied both by God and nature. Same sex people cannot have a natural family. Of course, an argument is made that judges are competing with their writings in hopes of being part of history, for their own fame rather than sound judgements. They, like scientists that want to have a breakthrough to be honored but don't have sound facts. The love aspect has questions, too. Love can come in many forms. I love my cat, and we will be together, no doubt, until death do us part. This does not mean we should be married. On the other end of the spectrum, an extreme- where a woman married a building in Seattle, Washington; complete with a minister. Another woman married the Eiffel tower. Still, the Supreme Court will decide if gay marriage will be the law of the land (not of God and nature) and I wonder how it is reasoned that somehow, a gay person's rights are being denied in the opposition to gay marriage. All people could always get married, it just had to be with someone of the opposite sex. In fact I see that the majorities' right of the pursuit of life, liberty and happiness is being infringed upon. Why must they be left without a word that specifically describes their bond to satisfy the desire of the minority of gays. The word marriage will no longer describe that bond of male and female. Marriage has always had to do with the union of two different types of people. What female hasn't looked at men and said how different they are, and men notice how women, too, are different. When I discussed Lou-deanne in the beginning of this writing, I can remember how intrigued I was with her just because of our differences, and the differences between man and woman are obvious to anyone that cares to look. En masse it is amazing that two creatures that are so different decide to join for life. Intrinsic is that attraction that to take away its immutable definition of the joining of the two would be detested by many. I see if you want to be different then you will be treated differently, no matter what the topic is. Even though my gay friend said we are all the same, I had to state, "no, we are not. You are attracted to men and I am attracted to women." Although some try to make this a small difference, it is in fact a big difference. Men being with men or women being with women can more accurately be described as a close friendship. If you take sex out of the equation, it is the same as two girlfriends, or two guys who are best friends. They enjoy their time together, pal around and may even live together. When it is man and woman together, it's a whole different set of circumstances. Therefore, it deserves its own word.

It wouldn't be an issue for many if society had a clear view of the gay marriage dilemma. Court rulings have come in with three judges voting one way and two the other.

States have OK'd same sex marriage and then repealed it, then reinstated it. Maine voted it down then voted it in by a slim margin. Vermont had a "bring Vermont back" backlash where people even painted that slogan on the side of their barn to try to go back to the traditional definition. States had addressed the issue on their own and defined marriage as between a man and woman, clearly showing the will of the representatives of the people, only to have their laws struck down by a federal judge. Just think of all the people involved to declare the will of the people in those states and then have their work negated by just one person. Even if gay marriage is enacted, it doesn't represent the will of the people. Even many gays are against calling same sex union marriage.

This is all about the definition of a word. Nowhere is it a suggestion before the court that gay people should have another designation such as civil unions or registered partnerships, which has been the path most nations have taken…. such as Australia, Ireland, Germany, instead of same sex marriage. (This is among nations that recognize it at all.)

It must be observed that in looking at a map of the world, same sex marriage is only accepted by a small number of nations. The vast majority do not recognize it, and approximately one third of the world have laws that range from a large penalty to life in prison to death. I am not even for anything legal that gives non male/female relationships any benefits. Back in the simpler days, men went out to work, women stayed home to take care of the home or raise kids and there was even company for the dog. The man would get benefits from his employment, the woman would be given his pension if he died to take care of herself since she spent her life in the house. Now people are lucky to get a pension at all. Wives are forced out of the house to work to support the family, the kids get less attention and the poor dog suffers because he is a pack animal and he is forced to stay at home by himself. Though life has many home scenarios, this first one was, and probably still is, the ideal situation. Gay marriage will in many situations take money out of my pocket in the form of benefits to joined partners. I could see it in a normal marriage because of the promotion of the traditional family unit; a necessary social formation for the proper continuation of the human race.

Affront not only to me, but to many that do not agree with the alternative lifestyle, is that I do not want to see any of my money going to support a lifestyle that unfortunately, especially male/male, causes so many health problems. Without going into detail, it is known that what they do together the human body was not designed to do. University of Virginia Health says LGB people experience higher rates of asthma, headache, allergies, osteoarthritis, GI problems, sexual violence, alcoholism, mental health illness, cancer, cardiovascular disease, obesity, hepatitis B and C, urinary tract infections, and sexually transmitted infections… and transgender people face higher risk of emotional and physical abuse, physical and sexual violence, sexually transmitted infections, viral hepatitis and HIV and substance misuse. 40% have attempted suicide. Consequences such as AIDS, STDs, etc. are experienced, even mental stress and anxiety..and then there are the innocent wives that get aids from their bisexual husband, or like in my family commit suicide because they couldn't take all the mental baggage that went with it. I don't even want to write about it, and can't imagine the avoidable stress they go through.

Money takes stage in another issue with the fight for gay marriage. Some say it is about getting money for them, that benefits are the only motivation and they are fighting hard for gay marriage. Amazing too, is the fact that prisoners demand the jailers to let them change their sex while in prison with the cost being paid by us.. A prisoner in a military trial was found guilty in the wikileaks disclosure of "sensitive information." He threatened to castrate himself if he was not allowed to transform into a female. I'm sure there are a lot of people in and out of the military that would be glad to castrate him for free since he was a traitor- the most detestable crime a soldier can commit on his fellow soldiers. The case is not isolated either. State prisons are paying for this also. It's amazing, the state will put up the money and effort because someone says,
"I am a woman in a man's body." Well you know what? I am a rich sophisticate in a poor common man's body. Can the state put up the funds to change that? I mean I feel sorry that these people have such a tortured mind and suffer from their thoughts, but is that the best way to deal with it? Wouldn't it be more realistic to tell them, "Hey, you're a guy, get over it." If not, you're leaving the door open for any fantasy that someone wants to entertain. What about all the other people with less than traditional relationships? Polygamists, pedophiles, necrophiliacs, those who commit incest and bestiality, people who have loving and sexual attractions to amusement rides. Doesn't acknowledgement of

equal rights make other groups' desire to pursue their interests more legitimate? One could even say that polygamists have more of a right to practice their beliefs since it is men and women involved instead of same sex people. What is socially acceptable? History has sanctioned sexuality in the past and even has problems currently in defining boundaries. Prostitution, though between a man and woman, has been accepted by Canada but not the US. (The US only has a few counties in Nevada where it is legal). Society sets boundaries of what is acceptable and what is not. Even though prostitution, like homosexuality, has been around forever, that should not make it acceptable. Leviticus writings 3500 years ago not only showed us that homosex was judged as improper back then but shows it existed back then. It is not going away. Our society has to decide whether legitimizing the behavior by granting marriage to them is an acceptable path to take, thereby degrading the traditional marriage. Other relationships aren't accepted. We didn't want marriage to be degraded by allowing multiple wives or husbands. We don't mind denying two closely related people being married, no matter how much love they have for each other. So denying homosexuals marriage is not all that far-fetched of an idea.

We are leaving our children with a world of no morals. Television has programs with prostitutes talking about how they are pursuing their profession and that there is nothing wrong with what they are doing. We are indoctrinating children to think that whatever path they choose to pursue is ok as long as it doesn't take away from their self-esteem.

Children are told that their actions or the actions of others are ok and we must love everyone and everything, and that we shouldn't judge people. We do judge people….constantly. Some people judge people all the time, it is their job. We call them judges. All the decisions we make are based on our own judgments. In my admiration of Lou-Deanne, it was my choice to pursue her. It is everyone's choice to do whatever they decide to do. Is it right that we don't set guidance for the children to give them bearings in life. Shouldn't we? We should introduce the right choices to nurture them in a direction that will enhance their lives in a beneficial way.

Not too long ago I was listening to the radio and a very young girl was talking about how she was talking to her friends about "today, I might feel like a girl and tomorrow I might feel like a boy, what difference does it make?" I think she will find that it does make a difference. More importantly, it was adults that gave her the guidance to come out with those statements. Why are parents projecting these non-traditional beliefs on their children when there is a greater chance of them being straight as they mature. Why not give guidance along traditional lines and if they naturally develop homosexual desires then let them develop from there. Now it seems children are being conditioned to a gay lifestyle.

Another young child could talk like a professor about homosexuality and development. The boy became a girl before high school and certainly had mannerisms and spoke like a female. When looking at the videos of her as a very young child, she was shown dressing up in girls clothes and had makeup on. Well I can see her parents didn't necessarily lead her on a normal path. Children can't go over and buy their own makeup and buy a dress. I can't help but think that the parents led the child on (maybe unconsciously) to question what gender they were.

I have to say that dressing up as a woman does not make you a woman, but social conditioning determines your development, along with natural instincts. That is why it is so important to have traditional families with role models of both sexes present in the house. Single parenting, which is in most cases going to be the mother, exposes a young male to an environment dominated by female culture.

Having bumps on your chest does not make you a woman. Wearing a dress and stockings and high heels does not make you a woman. Wiggling while you walk and talking in a high pitch does not make you a woman, and playing with dolls does not make a child a girl. My young friend and I were observing an extremely feminine acting guy. He was fortyish but talked like a fifteen year old girl. My friend commented that he was acting more feminine than a girl. It seems like so many are acting, and some are really bad actors. Transgender people change with hormone treatments. If hormones are necessary then to say you were the other sex in the beginning was false; you used chemistry to change yourself.

It's tough.. it's tough to survive in this world,...sometimes it's hard just to get through a day. Our habits determine our daily routine and our approach toward the future. Habits can be changed. Studies show that a small percent of people who dabble in homosexuality actually continue. An interesting annotated essay on the topic is *What causes homosexual desire and can it be changed?* By Paul Cameron.

Don't take writings disapproving of gay behavior as hatred toward gays. I don't support that. It is just that the behavior is not only against my beliefs but isn't even imaginable by me. We can still care for other human beings without supporting their lifestyle. We could even encourage them to change their ways. I love my cat, but some of its behaviors are incomprehensible. I might try to get her to change her ways and redeem herself but I'll still care for her like she's my child. I don't look at my writing as a hateful movement or endeavor. I took sociology in college and am still fascinated by the study of the development, structure, and functioning of human society. It seems gays are putting a real effort to be accepted, especially with the always "ready for a cause" youth. All people should be approached on an equal, caring, friendly basis. It is our choice of conduct which makes others get close or further away. Why I am concerned about gay marriage fascinates some of my friends that are of the "why do you care?" camp. I feel comfortable to say, I do care about the outcome of abandoning marriage as we have known it ....enduringly as our recognition of the bonding of woman and man. Others have said marriage is not just between human beings. It is a relationship rooted in human nature and governed by natural law. Same sex marriage makes couples less accepting of marriage for procreation. Countries that support same sex marriage have lower birth rates. Canada, the Netherlands and Sweden's birth rate hovers around 1.6 children per woman, well below the replacement rate of 2.1.

Same sex marriage will institutionalize that children do not need a mother and father making the dissolving of a normal marriage more plausible. Much like abortions and contraception in the 1960s made men feel they could leave a woman and child because the mother could have used contraceptives or gotten an abortion. Same sex marriage will impose its acceptance on all of society. By legalizing same sex marriage, the state becomes its official and active promoter. The state calls on public officials to officiate at the new civil ceremony, orders public schools to teach its acceptability to children and punish any state or local employee or even private citizens who expresses disapproval.

In the private sphere, objecting parents will see their children exposed more than ever to this new morality (immorality?), businesses offering wedding services will be forced to provide them for same sex unions, and rental property owners will have to agree to accept same sex couples. In every situation where marriage affects society, the state will expect the religious or those with morals to betray their religion and conscience by condoning, through silence or act, an attack on the natural order and religious morality.

And of course what would be the reason for gays to marry? Property and legal issues can be contracts and other laws. How are rights being denied? They can form a legal union and get all the rights of married couples so how are they being discriminated against?

The previous were my writings in 2015. It's 2024. It's amazing how the analysis of things change in time…..and how crazy things have gotten. In my lifetime opinion on transsexuals went from a form of insanity to acceptance…well acceptance by some. Kids are telling their parents to put bowls on the floor for them so they can eat out of them because they identify as an animal ... and the parents do it. Young boys are being told to leave the girls alone and being gay is okay. School dress codes are almost non-existent, and young kids are killing each other for their sneakers. Young girls are suing surgeons because they cut their breasts off when they were in high school, because at the time they wanted to be boys. Female only bathrooms…a thing of the past. Have you had enough of this stuff yet?

This writing started as a friend of the court letter to the Supreme Court before they voted on gay marriage. I was certain that they would not approve of it because the distinction between a gay marriage and a traditional marriage would not have been established. Interestingly the vote was four to five as close as if you get in the Supreme Court. Just one vote would have made it so that gay marriage would not have been voted in. The justices that voted against gay marriage had compelling and logical explanations as to why it should not have been made law. Their opinions are easily searchable. Surprising to me is not only the decision, but what has transpired in the last 10 years. A town clerk went to jail because she refused to issue marriage certificates. A cake baker was fined for not baking a cake with a gay theme and that case went to the Supreme Court where the 5-4 decision went in his favor. 36 countries out of 195 countries of the world allow same sex marriage (17% of the world's population). LGBT has become LGBTQQIP2SA. …so far….Some put a + in there, and whatever else I don't know… I thought the plus was going to handle it all. It is also odd to me that all these people who group themselves together actually have nothing in common. A pride parade consists of so many different kinds of people that have nothing in common. Let's take the initialism LGBTQQIP2SA. Lesbians are two girls, gays are guys, T's are transsexuals. Then the questioning, queers, intersex, pansexuals, two spirit, and ally. Some have no sexual feelings at all. Truthfully, I do not understand what all those things mean. It gets so convoluted. But evident is that they're all different and don't have anything in common except for the fact that they are not what might be considered normal, traditional, or straight. It seems to me also that many of them have another trait: they're exhibitionists. A girlfriend of mine and I decided to take a trip to Provincetown Massachusetts which is known as a LGBT+ capital. There we observed a good number of men that were walking around in wedding gowns. It was the thing that summer. It was sort of shocking at first to see someone walking down the street in a wedding gown with a nice body and you just want to see what the bride looks like, and then they turn around and there's a guy with a beard. A group of them were sitting at a table at a roadside cafe. I told my friend I have to get a picture of them. No, she said, expressing fear that they would be upset about it. I said no, they're exhibitionists, and I asked their permission to take their picture. They not only obliged me but posed …complete with roses in their teeth. Such is a mindset that conducts their life with the intent of gaining attention. A gay pride parade is an exabitioalist's dream. Kids just join the party….and what are they proud of?

Of course everyone is different. It's hard to understand that mindset if you're not involved in it.

My aunt could not have children so she acopted a boy with my uncle. My cousin Billy developed into being a homosexual. My aunt talked about it in her extremely old age. Billy had long since died of AIDS, along with my brother and step brother. My aunt did a lot of talking in the last month of her life and I guess it was important for her to talk about her homosexual son. She loved him and even changed her church affiliation to one that would be accepting of homosexuals. She said that she could never understand homosexuality. Even with all the years she'd had her own son she just couldn't. She said her son couldn't understand transsexuals. Bill could understand homosexuals, and straight people but he just couldn't understand transsexuals. That's proof positive that we all have our limits, and just in our understanding of things we make boundaries.

   Transsexualism came into the spotlight in the last 10 years too and Bruce Jenner was the poster boy. He won the decathlon (the super male competition) setting a world record during the 1976 Olympics in Montreal. Vanity Fair had him on the cover and he won woman of the year even though he transitioned less than a year before. Such is Hollywood. Such is sensationalism that sells magazines and promotes television award ceremonies. But I mentioned Bruce mostly because of the fact that he was in the news again recently. He objected to transsexual males competing against females and agreed with a Mineola New York decision not to let that happen there. He said that it would ruin girl's sports ... .and as an Olympic champion who had received all the benefits of advertisers money he knew that they would have been deprived of financial gains too. So there you have it, a transsexual saying that premales should not compete against real women. We all have our parameters. He's not the first either. Renee Richards, the male tennis player that hopped the net, stated that he had benefit over his competitors because he was at one time a male. This is a big deal when you look to see how much women have suffered over these sex changed men competing in women's sport. A mixed martial arts female fighter said she had never been hit so hard as when she was hit by a transformed man. High school, college, and professional sport…even the Olympics…have deprived women of their recognition after their lifetime of training. Then, move to the dressing room where at gyms and female bathrooms the anatomically correct men waltz in under the guise of being imagined women and they expose themselves to women and female children who tell stories of being frightened to death. Can women…especially women… not have privacy and security. That's why I got so involved in all this….it's gotten out of control. High school females shouldn't have to complain about males being in their showers (and then be told it's legal and they are wrong for complaining). It's out of control.

Another thing that came to light about Bruce was that his family was not necessarily very happy about the fact that he transitioned. That situation is not unique to Bruce. Family members can be embarrassed and suffer anxiety over such things. In many ways it's a self-centered act…and one that not everyone's happy that they did. One man transitioned then after years of living as the different sex said "what am I doing" and transitioned back. Interestingly he said that people who say that they were "born that way" were not accepting personal responsibility for their actions.

It might be titillating to do such things but it takes its toll on society. My friend Susan had a business and had a gay employee. When he left her employ he turned in his computer and for a charitable donation she gave it to her son's Christian school. When it was first opened in class there were pornographic pictures for all the kids to see. She said her son never lived that down. Then as a side story she said she used to wear all kinds of colorful jewelry. Bright, vivid coral and jewel pins. She said she had to stop wearing them because everyone thought she was wearing some kind of gay pride flag arrangement and she didn't want to identify with that.

Most people just want to go on with their own lives and really don't care what other people do. What bothers them the most is that so many gay people have this in your face attitude. They can't just live their own lifestyle but feel they have to flaunt in front of others…. which they can, but others are going to judge them and in most cases they just want to avoid them, adding to the loneliness and depression that many feel. Our town had a school superintendent that was gay. His first interview he made it very clear that he was. He also told how he sued the other school districts that he worked for because he was fired for being gay. It didn't end well for our town either.

Too many people for whatever reason are trying to promote homosexuality. In Washington state there's a new curriculum coming to Washington's public schools starting in the 2025 school year. Senate Bill 5462 will mandate that students learn about the contributions of underrepresented groups in school including those in the LGBTQ+ community. Why mention sexuality at all? A poll after the article had results of 92% of readers against the bill. In 2020 Nickelodeon announced SpongeBob was part of the LGBTQ community. SpongeBob is geared to six to 11-year-olds. If that's not indoctrinating children to the gay lifestyle I don't know what is.

Let's face it, all kids are inquisitive. They will experiment and get involved in whatever they are exposed to. It's no wonder that suicide is the third leading cause of death in young people's 15 to 24. Life's gotten too complex for them. Priorities for the education of children have been distorted. It's odd that some can name every variation of sexual preference but can't make change. They are being exposed to too much too often. Shouldn't kids be filling their minds, time and conversations with more than discussing sexual identities and the complex baggage with esoteric explanations?

The idea of inclusion and diversity has the opposite effects of what it was meant to do. Diversity doesn't bring people together. Diversity doesn't create unity, it creates separation. Conformity creates unity. Diversity creates confusion, conflict. Here in my local school I can imagine that diversity is causing so much conflict. There is a huge international representation of the student body. You can't tell me that when children go home to their Jamaican parents that they're going to be told that it's okay to think that gay people are okay. Many European, East European and Middle East nations have a large representation where religious morals are a part of their upbringing. Logic will bring us to the fact that such beliefs are going to cause many heated discussions both in classrooms and out in the halls or the playgrounds. It pulls them apart. Conformity is what brings people together. The inclusion factor was to bring marginal kids into the fold. But now it's had the opposite effect in that non-marginal kids, kids with traditional morals and upbringing, are meant to feel alienated. Like George Carlin said "Can't kids just be kids anymore." I personally know some very diverse people that you wouldn't want to include in anything. All this talk of diversity doesn't include ideas like mine, so here is no inclusivity. It's just a set of talk and actions to make people think that everyone gets along. The more realistic view would be that they can have their playground and I can have mine. They stay in their lane, I stay in mine. You do you and I'll do me. I can't see a well bred child with high morals being the one that is excluded and chastised now. Quite possibly all those that have been woke for such a long time should take a nap, recharge as only sleep can do and rethink their mind and thoughts. Why have we found it so important to divide ourselves by designating ourselves as one thing or another?

GAZA

My interest in Gaza started in my interest in the news...to know what is going on. "Problems" in the Middle East have been going on my whole life. I remember as a child being in awe as the Israelis won the Six Day War against all its Arab neighbors. I rooted for them, the underdogs. For as long as I remember...for some sixty years, the coverage of Arab/Israeli relations portrayed Israel as the innocent, righteous and persecuted nation. Much of my view I attribute to the media coverage that brainwashed me and others to believe the guiltless Israel deserves our support and sympathy. I kept that attitude for most of my life as I went about living as most do with the concentration on my own endeavors, caring little about, much less having the time, to ponder international politics. As age tempered my invincible attitude, I progressed to be more caring of all people in the world and the lives we all must live. I took note of the song lyrics "we have all sweated beneath the same sun...and looked up in wonder at the same moon" that we were all alike. I tried to get the other's view and what others are dealing within their lives. Priorities changed and my seeking of knowledge increased. The news of thousands of people in Gaza being killed by Israelis turned my head and I looked into it.

Your views on the Palestinian-Israeli conflict depends on where you enter the circle of events that seem to go in rotation. Israel takes land and breaks agreements with the Palestinians so the Palestinians fire rockets into Israel. Israel responds with superior strength and invades Gaza, killing Palastinians in what could be seen as a blood bath. Hence Israel is bad, aggressive, and a hostile nation. Or, you see the Palistinians fire rockets into Israel. Israel defense forces respond by an invasion of Gaza. Many (Palistinians) die as Israel attacks those responsible and many innocent civilians are killed. Land is confiscated by Israel to secure areas in the West Bank. A view of Israel defending itself from the aggressive Palistinians can be seen.

The big picture is that almost two million people are in Gaza which the Israelis supervise like a prison camp. Palistinians cannot leave. They cannot export anything; they cannot import anything but are restricted to items allowed by Israel. The Gaza Strip is essentially a concentration camp which is unimaginable considered what the Jewish people went through during World War II. It is barbaric not only for the amount of years that it has been going on but also for the disregard for human life as protesting, defenseless Palistinians are gassed and shot.

As long as I have been meaning to write about this I thought maybe it would be settled. Peace would be worked out and the area would settle down. For 64 years I have been waiting for an end to the violence. I prayed for a seemingly impossible event like the taking down of the Berlin wall and the uniting of the Germanys. That the walls built to contain the Palistinians and separate them from the Jews would come down and peace would ensue. When will the killing stop? How can it go on? It's baffling that the cause of the violence is attributed to two different religions, practiced by Jews and Muslims, who both have the same God. That God commands them not to kill. Aren't they ashamed to dishonor God? Can they not stop for God's sake? Possibly a religious compromise will work because nothing seems to be working now. Days ago protests resulted in the death of an 8-month old child and 60 other people because they were protesting the opening of the U.S. Embassy in Jerusalem on May 14th, 2018. It was moved under orders from the Trump administration and was a "slap in the face" to the Palestinians. Jerusalem was supposed to be a split city controlled by both the Israelis and the country of Palestinian … a country that is always supposed to be acknowledged but never is. Agreements were always made to develop a two state settlement to this perpetual crisis and those agreements were always broken… and the Israelis took more land and restricted more Arab movement. Interestingly enough, other nations' dignitaries did not attend the embassy opening in silent protest..

Palistinians are accused of being violent and uncooperative when in fact Israel uses every opportunity to slow… then stop… then put in reverse the steps made toward peace. I see the desperation of the Palestinian people when they stand up to their captors. They throw stones at massively armed Israeli troops knowing that they may be killed by them as they have in the past. They have a "what do I have to lose?" attitude. If nothing is done, nothing will change. Standing defenseless while taunting Israeli troops seems suicidal. It's the frustration of captivity, broken agreements and prosecution that promotes this seemingly insane behavior.

Like the American Indian the Palistinians have seen their land confiscated. They have been put on the reservations and had treaty after treaty rescinded. I wonder if the future will bring that some of the Palistinians follow the way of the American Indian and will open casinos in the West Bank and Gaza and fund themselves to a prosperous life that way.

Something has to be done. For generations now the Palistinians have been captive, tortured and deprived of human rights. It's been going on for such a long time that it isn't even publicized much when Palistinians are killed. Sometimes I search for just one story on the major news internet sites when I know that some Palistinians have died and I have to do a lot of looking to find something written about it. It's like it's hidden, or trying to be played down…. not headline news anymore.

I am an American and the United States has the distinction of being one the two major places in the world that Jews live, Israel being the other. Here Jews influence politics as can everyone else. Some powerful, rich, persuasive Jews have laid down the groundwork and perpetuated the theory that the Arabs persecute and attack the Isralis. That Israel is only defending itself. (They don't have an "Army" but instead call their military a "defense force")… but time after time the violence is started by Israeli attacks which are prompted to prevent the enemy from having an advantage. I had the honor, time and horror of reading my Christian Bible pretty much from cover to cover. Reading it I was shocked that the Promised Land was inhabited before the Israelis arrived and the promise of wells and housing already there was because people lived there…and the promise of the promised land was only accomplished because the Israelis killed every inhabitant of

the land and took everything over. The biblical stories were barbaric, shocking ...to see
what people would do in the name of God to fellow humans.

As time went on the Israeli presence in Jerusalem was replaced by another group of
people then by others. The jews dispersed around the world and then after world wide
oppression Ben Goin started a jewish homeland movement where droves of jews were
returning to their "homeland". With bombings and force the jewish zealots invaded
Palestine for a second time. Similarly to the first, without regard for the inhabitants and
under the authority of their bible, through violence and manipulation they managed to
take over the area and contain the previous residents in an inhumane way that resembles
incarceration.

Israeli separatist strategy resembles the black/white separatist policies of segregation
only with a torture aspect thrown in to the mix. With such conditions it's no wonder that a
Palestinian set himself on fire as a protest. Like Budist monks, setting yourself on fire is
pretty much as desperate as you can get to prove your point.

What effect has the protesting accomplished? Years of travel restrictions have
devastated the Palestinian economy and blocked access to schools, family visits, and
medical care. Unemployment is at 65% for young people and 49% overall. 80% for
young women. All this punishment and the Palistinians go on. Oddly the US and Israel's
refusal to deal with Hamas after they were voted into power by the Palistians backfired.
The restrictions of food and trade in an attempt to oust Hamas actually gave more support
for Hamas. Hammas set up a lucrative trade system via tunnels under the Egyptian
border, hired the unemployed and made themselves respected by the Palistians. Like
Colombian drug cartels who helped the local people, Hamas got respect by enriching
people's lives. Why haven't the Israelis and their big brother the United States gone that
route? Work towards a mutual benefit. Now the US under Trump's watch is threatening
action and taking funds away from the Palestinians, stating that they will go on with their
own settlement of hostilities with their own peace plan without the benefit of Palestinian
representation. No wonder 40,000 Palisinas charged the border fence in protest last
month. That's not a mob, it's a human wave of desperation. Peace talks have been stalled
for four years now and what does the US do to help- nothing. They move the US embassy
to Jerusalem to make things worse. Maybe if the US wasn't so pro Israel progress would

be made. As in the past Israel actions were so egregious last month that the international organization Human Rights watch said the use of lethal force during these current events constitute war crimes. After all there were 3100 wounded and approx 120 killed. Hopefully world pressure will make things move along in the middle east for the benefit of all. Input from all nations should shape the region, not just the United States. It is through the major involvement of the US that Israel has progressed as much as it has over the years. Armed by superior US weapons and intelligence it has been able to be established, develop, expand and become a vigorous, rigorous and determined national representation of the Jewish people. Their intelligence shows in what they have accomplished in their self declared section of the world in such a short time. People united under the power of their God can achieve amazing things. Look how the mostly Christian United States took over much of North America and expanded further all under Manifest Destiny. It is a great motivator to know God is on your side and you are fulfilling his will. Nations have rallied their people with religion in the past and will no doubt in the future. It would be wonderful if we could find a way for the world to unite for the common good so desperately needed in our current world. People, united under their king, their chief, their pharaohs, their flag, God or their nation. How much towards what is right could be accomplished for our fellow man as well as ourselves? Will it happen in our lifetime? Ever? Or are we humans so self centered that there will always be those who want their way and nothing else? Palestinians have been obstinate in their actions too. They refused to acknowledge Israel as a nation for what seems like forever. Now the Israelis don't want to recognize the Palistians in solutions that were agreed to in the past. It seems they are happy with the status quo. I don't think that it can continue forever as it is but I felt the same way forty years ago. Israel consistently states that they are not at fault, no matter how clearly they acted in the wrong. It's almost laughable sometimes when they deny fault when their own version closely shows they are at fault. I sometimes laugh even though it is so tragic how some situations work out.

   Things are changing ….not quickly but slowly. The United Nations gave Palestine a seat in their assembly which gave them some recognition as to being a nation of their own. They can't vote, but at least they are recognized. Then too, younger US citizens are more supportive of the Palestinians. Whether it's because of more fairness in news reporting or they're increasing intelligence, it's a move towards a more just understanding of the Middle East. Certainly more people are writing and more importantly being published and distributed to present a more realistic understanding of what is happening there. Now daily actions by the Israelis and their defense force spurs me on to write. Even some Israelis are talking about how horrible their government's actions are.

  Palestinians get a lot of support which leads to a rearmament of rockets and rifles...arms and supplies of all kinds. Much of what continues the cycle of events is impossible to stop. Phycologically...on both sides is the remembrance of those who have died. On both sides resentment sets in and revenge emerges. Who can find it easy to forgive and forget the fact that someone killed a loved one. A child, mother, father, brother and sisters, friends have been killed and leave a heartbreak in so many people's hearts, on both sides. It reminds me of "The Troubles" in Northern Ireland that seemed to go on forever (and maybe still do) as revenge and resentment continued, attacks and killings made both sides unwilling to compromise. There, like in Palestine, there were barbed wire exclusion zones and military emplacements checking people here and there in their travels. I wasn't involved on either side, I had no connection to either side, but I had some Irish (and some English) descent and I hated the English. Such is human nature.

  There have been three major wars in Palestine in the last 10 years. 3284 Palistinians have been killed by Israeli 'defense forces' and 53 Israeli civilians have died. On the world stage funding by outside forces should be held accountable. Britain has sold over 400 million dollars in arms to Israel since 2014. Israel receives more military aid from the US than the US gives to other countries combined. Aid to the Israeli state from the US is in the tens of billions of dollars ...why I don't know. Israel is a prosperous nation. It ranks very high in many economic rankings. It has a growing economy, rising standard of living, and is among the better living nations of the world. Why is the US giving any aid at all? I feel as a US citizen that we are supporting in an excessive way a persecuting and oppressive Israeli Government, who now, in 2018, has declared Israel a Jewish Nation state (not one of both jews and muslims Arabs, and others- a jewish state) which has set up an environment like apartheid of South Africa's past where a separate but equal state exists and I am not sure how equal it is.

On the other side people are afraid to side with Palistinians because they do not want to side with a state that is perceived as terrorists. No one wants to do that. Meanwhile Israel allows Palestinian children as young as 12 to be jailed and between 500-700 Palestinian children are tried in the courts. Terrorism takes place in the flying of drones over Palistinians and Israeli troop movements, fencing in of civilians and watching their movement from guard towers. Just a jet flying over would terrorize me, especially with Israeli's attacks of the past. But terrorism has been part of the current Israelis seventy year occupation of Arab lands. During its formation in 1946 the King David Hotel was bombed - planned in part by Menachem Begin. Israel has a compulsory draft for 18 year old males and females. Males serve 2 years and 8 months and females serve 2 years. Certainly this reinforces a hostile mind set that began as they grew up. Essentially the nation is a military state with every citizen a soldier, retired soldier or a reserve.

The area is looking more like a fascist state with separation and no equality, the declaration of Israel being a Jewish state, and it seems all that is missing is a dictator. It is a disgrace that most know that Israel has no desire to make progress in the settlement of actions to determine Palestinian sovereignty and land borders. There is no reason for Israelis to do so; in fact only deterrents in the effort to possess all lands.

The status quo keeps Palestinians under their control. With any kind of Palestinian control Israel will be at greater risk. As things stand now the Palistinians are worse off now than since the 1960s. In negotiations the US has had to build back aid to get Israel to do anything. The 1956 Suez withdrawal, 1977 withdrawal from Lebanon, the Camp David Accord and in 1991 the withdrawal of a funds guarantee if Israel did not attend the Madrid talks. Now the US isn't holding back funds from Israel but aid for the Palistinains who need it most is being withheld…. to what end?

There is no comparison to the might of the parties involved. Israel is extremely more armed and powerful and decidedly in control. It's like David and Goliath in the Jewish bible with the Palestinians going up against the Israeli Goliath. There are not, however, similar results.

The great powers have always given more to the Israilis both in money, arms and moral support. Problems began with English withdrawl from the area amid terrorist activities by Jewish zealots and politics since then have kept Jews in control of the area.

Dedicated, smart, committed men and women who formed and now make up the Israeli army have shown resolve that have kept them with an upper hand , in a superior position and a controlling administration of the area. It is their desires that will lead the future.

As of August 14th 137 countries of the 193 member United Nations recognize the state of Palestinian. Israel refuses to support Palistinains and the rest of the world increasingly does. These past few months have been a miniature review of the conflict's history including a medical ship from Norway and manned by a multinational crew being turned back by Israel forces. Is this what Israel wants to be known as? A tyrant people? Ones who persecute, deny food, water, electricity freedom and human rights and dignity to others? The only way that this perception will change is if they change. Wouldn't they want to be known for their caring of their fellow man? For compassion, for negotiating a just solution and being a helping big brother? With an attitude change involving loving and caring they should get more loving and caring back. Even a more moral approach to fellow human beings would be desirable but simply being humane would change Israel's legacy to be something to be proud of. Peace in the Middle East should be based on trust, but no trust will be seen unless the words spoken are honest and caring. Human dignity is innate. To bestow dignity on our enemy is a beginning of ending hostilities. Israel is in position to end the grief, to leave a legacy of humanity and control the actions needed to create peace.

I would be remiss at this time of publication if I didn't add to these previous writings from 2018. A lot has happened since then, especially the October 7th 2023 actions by Hammas. The barbaric attack in Israeli territory has been described as another Holocaust. It has been said that it was Israel's 9/11.

There's another view never talked about. After writing about how the prison atmosphere that exists in the Palestinian territory of Gaza, could it be looked at as a prison riot? There are incredible similarities between that uprising and the Attica prison riot of 1971. There prisoners revolted because of poor living conditions including overcrowding, discrimination, and inadequate healthcare within the system. Of course they were incarcerated and were held in inhumane conditions. Hostages were taken and in the aftermath of gaining control the law enforcement killed hostages, fellow law enforcement agents and prisoners.

Israel's response to Hamas's actions could not be taken in any other way than an uncontrolled killing frenzy. Initial reports and subsequently, after months of fighting this so-called war, the casualties on either side were so lopsided that there is no way that Israel can describe it as defending themselves. The situation cannot even be described as a war. Figures as of March 5th 2024 were that over 30,000 Palestinians died to a total of 1,400 Israelis. Included in the dead were 94 journalists and 136 United Nations aid workers. Israelis were killing everyone. Israelis even killed some of the hostages that were surrendering with a white flag. The statistics are disgusting. The Israelis progressed under the guise of defending themselves when in fact they were committing genocide. Even South Africa, a nation disconnected from the conflict accused Isreal of just that…genocide. Other nations are in alignment. The International Court of Justice has found that Isreal is plausibly committing genocide. 70% of casualties of the Palestinians were children and women. 10,000 of the 30,000 were minors. 10,000 more are still missing under rubble. That doesn't even account for the innocent men that got caught up in the conflict. The physical damage done to the area of Gaza resulted in near total destruction of the country. 60% of Gaza has been flattened to the ground. Schools, hospitals, the infrastructure of water and sanitation were all destroyed. Now here at the end of March in 2024 the destruction and death continues. Added to that is the fact that aid is not getting into the Palestinians. They have no shelter and no food. They are starving to death ... and this is not the first time Israel has used starvation against the Palestinians.

Again I am disgusted as a US citizen for the fact that when a cease fire agreement and order was up before the United Nations the United States vetoed it letting the Israelis continue their murderous rampage. We continue to supply Israel with weapons. In February the US senate approved an additional 14 BILLION dollars to support Israel's destruction of Gaza. That's in addition to the normal 3 BILLION we contribute yearly in military aid. Italy, Spain and others have stopped sending arms to Israel. Do we, the United States, want to have the legacy of supporting mass murder? Are the Israelis looking to make their entry into the history books more disgusting than it already is?

The prisoners that revolted at Attica stated that they were not animals. They didn't want
to be treated that way. The way they were treated was inhumane and they just wanted to
be treated in a fair manner. That is what led to the revolt. Israel's confinement of the
Palestinians in Gaza has been going on for more than a generation. Some people there
have never seen freedom. Their international pleas went unanswered. Can the Israelis
relate their confinement in Egypt to the way they imprison the Palestinians in Gaza? Did
they not too want their freedom from Egypt? Israelis have been occupying Palestinian
land for the last 57 years. The UN has consistently accused Israel of war crimes. About
half of all UN resolutions that were issued specifically against a country have been issued
against Israel. That to me is an amazing statistic. I see that my questioning of Israeli
activities has been observed by others more scholarly than me.

Will this ever end? Will all that has happened be looked at sometime in the future as
some unbelievable chain of events as so much that is history is looked on now? Will
Israel's actions escalate things in the future? As they destroy Hamas will another group
emerge to continue the hate and fighting? Wouldn't it be prudent of Israel to work toward
peace?

FILITICIDE

Nothing shows in the eyes the love there is in the world better than grandparents
buying their grandchildren ice cream. I see it at my local lunch counter that is set up like
an old time soda fountain; the tin ceilings and all. The grandparents will put on a smug
looking face or sometimes expressionless, sometimes smiling in various degrees, but
always with sparkling eyes. Sparkling eyes are returned by the child and appreciation as
the ice cream is offered for their consumption and enjoyment. Ecstatic could be used to
explain the child's reaction. Joy, sometimes to the point of being emotional, exudes as the
reaction of the child as only a fat-sugar-salt composed food can. And there we have the
irony of the scene. The loving caring Grandparents are feeding the poor defenseless child
a combination of ingredients that have no greater purpose than to set them up for a
lifetime of addiction to unhealthy eating. An act done to contribute to the bonding of

generations turns out to continue an awful food consumption habit that has been plaguing society since our ability to indulge. There's nothing like eating, and taste has been a motivator as much as hunger. Scientists have counted the receptors on our tongues, their location, and our desire to consume tantalizing combinations of ingredients regardless of their health benefits or health detriments.

Naturally we are desirous of the ingredients that are causing havoc with our bodies. Back in the days of early human history we sought fat and sugars in our diets and consciously or unconsciously we still like its taste. Physiologically it was good for us to seek out these high energy food components in the past. It came with the protein-rich meat of animals that sustained our ancestors. With the physical exertion we endured in the past and the availability of fat in animals to fuel our bodies, the taste of fat was programmed into our makeup so that we still desire its taste today. The same with the fruit sugars. They too are high in calories and through technology are now concentrated well above what would be nature's portion.

Manufacturers know this and have actively pursued the development of desirable food stuffs by having scientists get just the right combination of fat, sugar and salt. These products have developed into a group known commonly as junk food. It's a big business. Some of the most affluent families and largest successful companies have made fortunes in feeding the public these healthless foods. Mars candies produced billionaires, Coca-Cola has become one of the most worldwide companies by selling basically liquid sugar. Whole chains of food stores …especially convenience stores …are filled with Twinkies, chips, Slurpees and in some there are just a few items that have any nutritional value at all. How convenient is that? Supermarkets have aisle after aisle of unhealthy foods. Our local store has 16 Isles but only three have real food in them. Aside from fruits, vegetables and fish what could be considered totally healthy? Reality is that consuming the vast majority of foods offered is unhealthy for you… is that right? When discussing Coca-Cola sales and its inherent high sugar … and its desirousness, one of my friends looked at me and said " it ought to be a crime to sell this"… and it should be. Ruthless businesses prey on human instinct and desires to present fake food which does nothing to nourish us …and in some conditions kills us.

I have a friend that I hadn't seen for years and he told me he had a heart attack. He was a super fit specimen of a human male. A professional scuba diver, avid snowboarder and hockey player. He said he was playing hockey when he got a stabbing pain in his chest... He knew he was having a heart attack and he drove himself to the hospital. He said he wasn't going to wait around for an ambulance to come since the hospital was less than a 10 minutes away. (Why he didn't just have someone else drive I don't know) but he said that because of bad weather he could not be flown to Boston for treatment. The doctor asked him if he could inject him with a drug that could cause him to die, to better survive his heart attack, and he responded "well what choice do I have." So he took the drug and eventually got to Boston and had another heart attack on the operating table. Obviously he survived and told me he had calcium build up on the arteries to the heart. The reason for this? He drank too much Diet Coke. Can you believe it? He tried to keep his weight down by drinking diet soda and it almost killed him. He said he did drink an awful lot of it and sometimes he just had diet soda during the whole day. How ironic to be doing something to benefit your health and then you almost die from it. Some diets are like that. You're supposed to lose weight or get some health benefit from eating something or not eating something else and it ends up causing you more problems. Usually someone wants you to buy something like a supplement or a diet plan or some secret thing that those in control are hiding and have something they don't want you to know. Reality is there just trying to make money off of you.

I walked the isles of a large grocery store and took note of what was there. Aisle after aisle were full of foods that were the only nutritional value was little or none. Even in the health food section there was a cleverly labeled product...one with a perfect picture and lettering to catch your eye... one with perfect convincing sentences to convince you of its healthy benefits. It turned out to have way too many added sugars. Then at random I picked up one health product after another and when I read nutrition labels I concluded that they weren't at all what they seemed to be.

Many things we thought were good about certain things are now being disproved. I was disappointed when they changed the limit of alcoholic drinks per day from two for a man and one for a woman to none for both. That's where science is now... none ...no alcoholic drinks... none. Alcohol, as well as its many downsides also causes Alzheimer's disease ...

and who wants that? Alcohol (among a long list) also causes cramps in older people's legs at night, gives them nocturia, dementia, and cancer. 40% of the people in prison for violent felonies were using alcohol at the time….55% of domestic abuse is attributable to alcohol. That should be eliminated for your health. Added to that, the sugars will help you develop diabetes.

The government should be criticized about all this too. The detriment to health that big business causes the public should be penalized. Cigarette manufacturers can't advertise to children and they have been sued successfully and strongly by people who have suffered from their products. Why should kids be targeted in advertising so they buy all this proven detrimental food? Adults too have been harmed and should seek damages. The food industry is using the same tactics that the cigarette companies did. They sabotage sound ingredient research conclusions by presenting research scientists and doctors (well paid research scientists and doctors) to refute negative findings and present their own products as safe and healthy ... .which they are not. They lie.

Also the government issues food stamps which allow people to buy all sorts of unhealthy food. At a Circle K in Maine (A Circle K is a gas station with a convenience store) I looked to find the shelves filled with junk food. The only thing of any nutritional value were bananas and some oranges. I couldn't believe the signs above the food in the aisles said that they were SNAP eligible. SNAP eligible signs were over all kinds of donuts, funny bones, fruit pies, strudel cakes, glazed donut sticks, fruit loops, pop tarts, Manchurian instant noodles, ramen noodles, assorted potato chips, Chex Mix, Doritos, Tostitos, fruity wiggly worms, gummy bears, M&Ms, goldfish, Chips Ahoy cookies, beef jerky, Dr Pepper, Mountain Dew, Pepsi, and Starbuck Frappuccino coffee to name more than a few SNAP eligible items. (government issued food stamps) SNAP stands for supplemental nutrition assistance program... and there's nothing nutritious in any of that stuff... Nothing. But there's plenty of innutritious things in them that are bad for us. They should be guiding people to only eat healthy food. If we did and people followed a healthy diet we would have less mental health issues, less cancer, less respiratory problems, less diabetes, less cardio problems, and people would live feeling better. I haven't seen a detailed diet plan yet that tells us what you should be eating. Perhaps the government or some humanitarian organization can distribute that plan at the stores so the majority of people are at least exposed to what healthy eating is. People get set in their eating habits and taste but if they are exposed and conditioned to eat healthy food they will find their taste and habits change and they will eventually enjoy healthy food.

Even with guidelines such as following the Mediterranean diet, a diet that has been proven to produce healthy longevity and prevent cardiovascular disease, you have to watch that you don't eat too many nuts and oils so that you don't gain weight. Interestingly enough the Mediterranean area is full of social people. This socialization can also add to longevity. Perhaps we should have the government promote socialization.

We should want to take care of ourselves. We are the one who benefits the most by proper eating and of course getting enough sleep and exercising. Results don't come without effort but they are worth it. My friend loves his Twinkies and Coke… and is unfazed that he has already had a toe cut off because of his diabetes. That's an addiction to junk food at its extreme. Another friend says he's going to eat whatever he wants and die happy... but he won't. There's more of a chance that he will die a slow and miserable death like someone who just wouldn't quit cigarettes and suffers slowly from emphysema. The only way he won't die slowly is if his poor eating gives him a heart attack and he dies instantly. (Which usually doesn't happen... You survive and lead a less enjoyable life usually with a physical or mental disability.)

There it is... There's no doubt about it, the efforts to pursue a healthy lifestyle results in a better future both physically and mentally and far outweighs the alternative.

The same is true for my friend who loves her wine. She jokes that she drank so much wine that her husband opened up a winery... which he did. As a true friend I told her we have to be careful about drinking ... the sugars there also contribute to diabetes and liver problems etc... her response?. She said "I know" and she opened up her blouse to show me her insulin pump which balances sugar in her body because diabetes had already taken over. (Or diabetes had already developed.)... And once you have diabetes...you have it. You have it for life….with no cure.

And then there was Huntly. He didn't have a clue his body was reacting to his poor diet and one day he just passed out. The doctors had to go to great lengths to keep him alive and afterwards to keep his eyesight and hearing. Some people similar to him have problems with their eyesight in which there is a progression of diabetes to cause blindness. They go through a routine with painful injections with needles in the eyes as treatment to prolong their vision. This diabetes is no joke. It's a terrible disease and mostly preventable.

There are so many examples of people not having self-control….even if it means their quality of life. They smoke cigarettes, use drugs,... there's a long list. But self-control is fortified by the desire of a quest for self-betterment. To feel better will motivate you.

Try this... Pick up 100 lb of something. Can't do it?... Try 50 or 20... Then walk around with it for as long as you can. When you finally put it down see how much better you feel. Lighter for sure, have more energy, are able to move easier, breathe easier. Life is more enjoyable without carrying around extra weight. The same would happen if you lost weight. You would change your body and mind in a positive way by having your blood pump better, increasing circulation of oxygen and letting your organs and your entire body work the way it was designed to do.. .to make you a better you. Unfortunately most of us have to lose weight, The statistics are staggering. Obesity not just being overweight but being 20 lb or more overweight. Obesity affects 42% of Americans. 17% of children 10 to 17 years old are obese.. and that number is growing. 26.8% of Maine is obese with 62.9 percent overweight. Just overweight statistics are at 35% of the population. 9.4 are severely obese which is 100 lb or more overweight. That's pretty bad. Here's the big statistic…. 70 to 75% of American adults are not at a healthy weight.

Our culture reinforces the bad habits too. Think of any festival occasion and you'll find treats. Cookies, bonbons, crossbones, cakes etc. Major occasions are synonymous with cross buns for Christmas, birthday cakes, Easter bunnies of chocolate with Halloween being the grand slam for kids. It's a candy day where they get so much candy it lasts a month or more. Let's not forget the ironic day... Valentine's Day, where to show we love someone by giving them insulin spiking candy... That's love? It works anyway. This guy I know would give girls candy which to me was creepy because the age difference was so great…. well he actually gave some to women of all ages, but the young girls loved it too.. Once I had a candy in my pocket and when I went to pay a bill at a bar I put it on the counter as I searched my pockets for cash…and the barmaid queried "Is that for me?". I gave it to her and made it a habit of bringing her chocolate every time I saw her and she literally ate that up. Then another time I gave the candy away since I didn't see her and that woman loved it. One good friend I confided in and told her that I hope she doesn't think it was creepy of me to give her candy and she said…"Never, it's never creepy to get chocolate" ….and that's how fortunes are made, loves develop, dentist prosper and children get jittery…and they get consumed in the desire for candy and form a bad habit.

We are responsible for ourselves and our kids but mass advertising makes the poison too tempting. The marketing is getting worse. Soda comes in super size bottles, shakes come with whipped cream on top now…how do you resist? The craving is so bad that desserts at restaurants are almost the same price as the meal, and we still get them. It's extremely hard to have self-control when the supply is handy and the desire is great.

Statistics on this matter are staggering. Diabetes is a disease. According to the Lancet, a peer reviewed medical journal, eating and drinking better could prevent one in five (that's 20%) of early deaths. Blood pressure is rising in children for the same reasons it does in adults- excess weight, poor nutrition, lack of exercise... Some schools do not even have physical education now in our negatively progressive society. Children used to be required to exercise... and of course that would improve social skills and socialization in general which is also lacking in our modern society. Cell phones, computers, texting, video games and many other electronic devices and their derivatives isolate people and expose them to weird behavior which they imitate and are further isolated by other children because they act... weird. When we try to get a good long happy life, socialization is one of the greatest contributors to that end. The US Health and Human Service had an article on Our Epidemic of Loneliness and Isolation. Our current society isn't socializing like it used to. Socializing is hard…if you act different you will be treated different. If you be yourself and be an individual you would be judged by your actions ... .and if you act in a way that bothers someone they will avoid you and criticize you, taunt you and possibly attack you... these are human traits that none of us can avoid. No matter how many laws are passed, no matter how you try to condition children to guide their actions, innate human responses will forever come out ahead even if it isn't what we ourselves want. So for social cohesion the electronic future seems to deter a necessary and healthy socialization by promoting isolation. I know it may seem that I am rambling and ranting in an effort to get my points across to you... so I continue to do so by saying... and I may be repeating things... we have to get back to eating real food.

Study after study has shown that since the 1970s the ultra processing of food has resulted in an increase of weight and related health issues. Some scientists and doctors and researchers say our mind and body cannot process what we are eating and cannot activate the digestive process properly. The 10,000 plus additives manufacturers put in processed food wreak havoc on our natural systems causing them to react unnaturally. Newer emulsifiers are altered and added to food which affects our microbiome the most. Emulsifiers are found naturally but the altered and designed emulsifiers cause cancer, leaky gut and destroy the normal bacteria, fungi, parasites and good viruses that normally coexist peacefully in a healthy person. This all is rooted in the fact that 70% of our food today is ultra processed. 2/3 of a child's diet contains unhealthy food...among other things caused by this fact is that children's cancer rate is skyrocketing which has been attributed to preservatives. Experts say today's food shouldn't be considered food at all because of its low nutrients and its harmful effects. Now the American diet has spread to Central and South America with stunning and observable outcomes... Historically fit people went from thin to fat in a decade and that's on a country level. From Kuwait to South America whole countries have exploded in size due to the American diet which is of course ultra processed food.

  How did we get here? As with many solutions the experts come up with in an effort to make people healthier, they instead made things worse. Fats in food were said to be bad and in some ways are but to get people to stop eating fat manufacturers started adding substitutes to satisfy the human feeling of taste. The go-to substance was sugar. Since then industrially processed food has surpassed smoking as a cause of death. The altering of food continues. All decisions of what is done in the food industry is made by major corporations. There's big money in food. We all have to eat. The companies are there to make money and do so by cutting costs. They are adding things to extend shelf life. They cut out costs in processing where they add unhealthy things to increase flavor, create flavor, and add to the customers addiction to the food. Much of the bad food is consumed by the lower end of the socioeconomics structure... you know... the poorer people...because all the cost cutting allows manufacturers to put the food on the shelves at a lower cost.

In 2023 41.9% of adults had obesity, 49.9% (that's half) of blacks, 45.6 of Latinos. 20% of children 2 to 19 have obesity .... a more than three time increase since the 1970s. In 2022 22 states in the US had adult obesity rates over 35%. A decade before no state had an obesity rate over 35%. Maine has 50% of their children overweight which is bad because they usually stay the same weight proportion that they had in high school. Casey King was a 33-year-old male that reached 845 lbs in weight. Casey is an example of what someone can do. He managed to lose 600 pounds... It took him 4 years. At 37 now he's down to 255. He is an example that anyone can do it if they set their mind to it. He said his weight was bought on by being a big kid and after high school he worked in restaurants and started eating even more. Several years later he moved in with his dad and his weight ballooned. He said his town had plenty of fast food restaurants but no healthy food choices. He has a point. Add it to poor people's perils. Some poor areas have food deserts, where there aren't any sources of groceries or healthy food stores.

Researchers figure that ultra processed foods have less nutrients than real food. Its nutrient deficiencies add to the cancers and other diseases that junk food promotes. Real food is what our diet used to be. Fresh fruit, vegetables, lean meat all of which isn't available except at grocery stores. Healthy foods are more expensive and require refrigeration and time to prepare and clean up after making meals. One researcher doctors' solution for nutritional health is to eliminate poverty. Then people will have money to buy the right food, prepare and store it. My reaction is that the people would have to be allotted money to do that and they would just spend the money by continuing their normal lifestyle and maybe use extra for other more destructive habits. People for the most part, can't manage money. It would be better to alot people healthy food....but what is hard for the masses to achieve is easier for an individual to achieve. They can reach the goal of healthy eating if they put their time and effort into it...as with most things if you put the effort into it you can achieve anything.

Shaming has become a discouraged way of handling things lately too. It used to be that friends, family, or anybody might comment on how someone was, or wasn't taking care of themselves. Out of love and caring people were telling others to watch their weight. Now we have positive body coaching for girls. The idea is to feel good about themselves and celebrate their extra weight. Some people are promoting body positive acceptance mainly because airlines are charging the overweight for two seats. They also have activist action by having fat girl gatherings and body positive meetings. They have overweight girl nights at nightclubs. Men can be any size to get in there. Oversized clothing is being advertised also. The attitude towards fat people is changing. There are even overweight beauty contests (Miss Plus). Their solution is to love yourself the way you are. Doctors are concerned this approach will deter efforts to have people follow a nutritious and healthy diet.

Being fat is not the only indicator of being improperly nourished. Sometimes there aren't any symptoms. An Australian woman who was young, pretty, active, fit looking, and felt fine, had her sugar addiction cause her blood work to be off the charts... she was on her way to becoming a diabetic.... which again is irreversible. On going to fast food restaurants she said where else can I go that I don't have to cook? Don't have to do dishes? It is served fast and I don't have to pay too much. Going to KFC, Burger King, McDonald's - people think they are bulletproof and don't think of the consequences in 20 to 25 years of time. Even there in Australia 250,000 people die a year from diabetes. Dialysis treatment has gone up 10% a year in Australia at a cost of 50 to $100,000 per person. There's a clear link between carbohydrate and sugar consumption and diabetes. Diabetes has many complications. It is the number one cause of blindness in ages 20 to 70. Problems with circulation, coronary heart issues are all because of diet. High sugar in the blood is attributed to high triglycerides which make the blood stickier which increases the risk of clotting. That creases the chance of heart attacks and strokes. Even people who think they are eating well aren't.

Our society has an odd side to it. Even with all the health problems linked to restaurants we still have places like the Heart Attack Grill. There diners could get the quadruple bypass burger for free if they weigh 350 lb or more. Waitresses in nurses uniforms would serve burgers that had a calorie count of 9,983 calories. (about 5x the recommended daily intake) One customer had a heart attack at the heart attack grill...appropriately enough. The Physicians Committee for Responsible Medicine requested the closure of the restaurant in protest to its insanely unhealthy menu. We as normal humans throw all caution to the wind, abandon reason, proceed blindly and show the intelligence of a snail when making eating decisions. The heart attack grill serves 650 customers a day. On the other end of the spectrum are parents who spend $31,000 for their kids to go to boot camp style weight loss clinics. It's live in. It's strictly regimented. Food is monitored. They write down what they eat. They learn to live with hunger. The kids say a lot of their problems were not knowing what was in the food they were eating... how many calories they ate, how many carbs, how much salt. They didn't know how bad their lifestyle was. They exercise by walking and working out. They say they feel better and they feel good that they are accomplishing something and learning lifelong habits to stay healthy.

All the bad choices in our diet lead to insulin resistance, which can broadly be defined as a subnormal response to normal insulin concentrations. (insulin is a hormone) Blood sugar levels affect a lot including things resulting in fatty liver disease, chronic inflammation, high blood pressure, decrease of good HDL, increased triglycerides, increased weight and belly fat, decreased immune system, decreases the body's ability to clean out and causing cardiovascular disease, stroke, dementia, kidney failure, blindness and amputations, (causes most of the previous three) and inability to fight disease and infections. It is involved in 95% of the degenerative diseases and is the most costly and most devastating ... .producing a slower death... causing suffering with more poor quality of life, bad moods and lower productivity. The condition of insulin resistance is three times more deadly than cancer. Over 70% of people have this condition... and it is mostly preventable and for many- reversible and reduction of visceral fat is necessary to accomplish that. Again you have to eat real food with no ultra processed food, no additives. Not eating real food will knock your metabolism out of whack. No sugar or starch. By doing this you can reverse damage plus lower your carb intake. Avoid processed foods- sugar, vegetable oils, artificial sweeteners, alcohol, gluten, dairies, soy, corn and conventional meat and fried foods. According to Time Magazine six amazing body changes happen when you give up carbs. You start burning fat...immediately. You feel less hungry when not eating refined carbs. Hunger is satisfied by fiber and protein and healthy fats. Your stomach gets flatter. You slash your risk of diabetes. Your muscles get stronger. You have more energy. Five foods to avoid per a Harvard Nutritionist (apparently studying the brain) are One: Foods made with industrial and processed seed oils like soybeans or corn oil rapeseed (source of canola oil) and oils from cottonseed sunflower and safflower seeds. They contain high omega-6 fatty acids. Excessive omega-6 fatty acids can lead to inflammation of the brain. Avoid them to prevent dementia and keep your mind sharp. Two: Foods with added and refined sugars. As well as other things the sugar can lead to excess glucose which can cause memory impairment. Three: Processed foods... A diet of ultra processed food may shorten telomeres which are the caps on the end of our DNA. Longer telomeres tend to promote healthy cellular aging. Short Telomeres increase chances of degenerative disease early in life. Also consuming high amounts of ultra processed foods have been shown to promote depression. Four: Using artificial sweeteners like saccharin, sucralose, and stevia can increase bad gut bacteria which can negatively affect your mood. Asparagine has been associated with anxiety and causes oxidation which causes increased harmful free radicals in the brain. Five: An 18,000 people study found that a diet high in fried foods was linked to lower scores of memory and cognition.

How do we change this worldwide problem? That's especially hard for the United States. We have this stubbornness that we do whatever we want regardless of the consequences. Our unregimented society is evident with these statistics: 1.6% of people in Japan have tried recreational drugs other than alcohol. In the United States that figure is 50%. Our government has made little efforts to protect its citizens from this obesity epidemic... yet China, because of its political structure, has introduced programs (especially since 2009) that made it so that now the number one hobby that Chinese people enjoy is outside activity. This outside activity is something psychologists say is a way to recharge ourselves. We are made to be outside with nature during the day where the visual stimuli relax and charge the brain adding to a healthy being. The Chinese are especially targeting the young so as to create lifelong healthy habits… a possible benefit of an authoritarian government. In Sweden candy consumption is limited to Saturday which tradition was started In the '50s to fight tooth decay in children. The tradition has also been credited with the Swiss children's ability to manage money and plan for their financial future. Since we are so individualistic in our United States people have to take the initiative to improve their own physical being. This just leads to a more enjoyable life. Lists have been made of ways to stop the craving of unhealthy foods. Number one: Drink water. Hunger gets confused with thirst in our minds. Drinking water before meals also fills us up... and it is key to letting our bodies work as they should. You can die in 3 days without water... six at the maximum. Drinking water will help with weight loss. Number two: Eat more protein. It satisfies you... It quells your appetite... makes you feel full... longer. A study of teenage girls showed protein produced a reduction of cravings…a significant reduction. Protein will keep you from overeating. You should have protein at every meal. Increasing protein intake can reduce cravings by 60% and cut out the desire to snack at night by 50%. Number three: Distance yourself from the craving. A change of thought or surroundings can stop your cravings. Go for a walk, take a shower... get involved in something that grabs your attention so you stop thinking about eating. Some people chew gum which mimics eating. Number four: Plan your meals for the upcoming days. Change your current eating routine to healthy eating habits. You will eliminate spontaneity and wondering what you will eat. If you eliminate the need to think about what you want to eat you can stay on a disciplined diet. Number five: Avoid getting extremely hungry. That will lead to craving food. Eat at regular times and have a healthy snack at hand. By doing this you might not get cravings at all. Number six: Fight stress. Studies show women under stress eat significantly more calories and experience more cravings than non-stressed women. Furthermore stress raises your blood level of cortisol, a hormone that can make you gain weight... especially in the belly area. A simple plan to minimize stress is to plan ahead, meditate (or pray) and generally slow down in life. Number 7: I am not a big believer in supplements, but the claims of a new one has good claims to results that I'll add it in here. It's spinach extract made from spinach leaves. It helps delay fat digestion which increases the level of hormones that reduce appetite and hunger like GLP-7. Studies show taking 3.7 to 5 grams of spinach extract with a meal may reduce appetite and cravings for several hours. One study in overweight women showed that five grams of spinach extract per day reduces cravings for chocolate and other high sugar foods by 87 to 95%. Number 8: Get enough sleep. Your appetite is greatly affected by hormones that fluctuate during the day. Sleep deprivation disrupts the fluctuations and may lead to poor appetite regulation and strong cravings. Studies support this showing that sleep deprived people are up to 55% more likely to become obese compared to people who get enough sleep. Our bodies are designed for a simple existence and simple daily routine... not late shifts, partying late…sleeping in on your day off. For this reason getting a good night's sleep may be one of the most powerful ways to prevent cravings from showing up. Number nine: Eat right.... Proper meals. Hunger and lack of key nutrients can both cause cravings... So you have to eat proper meals at meal times. Thereby your body gets the nutrients it needs so you don't get cravings of hunger right after you eat. If you find yourself in need of food between meals eat healthy, whole foods for snacks. Fruits, nuts, vegetables, or seeds. Dry edamame is a good choice because it has protein and all the nine amino acids that are essential for nutrition. Number 10: Don't shop hungry…and don't shop for junk food. If you have cravings while shopping you have access to anything you want there in the store. Go shopping while full which eliminates those compulsive buys. If you don't buy the junk food you can't have it in the house when you get cravings at home. So don't buy anything bad. Number 11: Practice mindful eating. It teaches you to develop awareness of your eating habits, emotions, hunger, cravings and physical sensations. Mindful eating teaches you to distinguish between the cravings and actual physical hunger. It teaches you to choose your response instead of reacting thoughtlessly or impulsively. Eating mindfully lets you concentrate on eating - slowing down and chewing thoroughly. You should chew everything completely about 32 times. Hard foods take about 40 chews (like steaks) -softer foods … like mashed potatoes and watermelon take 5 to 10 chews. Chewing starts the digestion process by producing enzymes in the mouth and breaks down the food to smaller sizes which are easier to digest... which is how we were designed to eat. The slower eating time also lets the brain pick up that we have eaten.... it takes 20 minutes for the stomach to let the brain know we have eaten enough. After you have eaten wait... you will feel full. Don't be distracted while you are eating... by the phone, TV... concentrate on your refueling.

50% of people experience craving. So we are not alone. Cravings play an important role in gaining weight, food addiction and binge eating. Following the tips on this list such as eating more protein, planning your meals and practicing mindfulness will allow you to take charge the next time cravings try to take you over.

Food cravings and smell go hand in hand. Marketers use synthetic smells around stores. They artificially duplicate the smells of cinnamon buns, burgers, popcorn, ice cream, waffle cones, etc, using aroma marketing for restaurants like McDonald's and stores like 7-Eleven. The smell of bacon will lure someone in like an earthworm for a trout.

Psychologists say that comfort foods that remind us of the security of grandmother's kitchen are our go to foods when we are stressed... The baked goods-pies, cookies and the like are the things to devour after a stressful day. It makes us feel less lonely and isolated. Pasta and its sauce are dived into after an unusually busy day. Our nose picks up the aroma in the room. The nose sends the information straight to the brain. Smell is the most delicate of all the senses. Chocolate is another tempting food smell. 50% of American women admit to serious chocolate cravings on a monthly basis before their cycle. Doctors say the desire for chocolate is due to three things. Hormone fluctuations, stress response in the brain and pleasure release from eating the chocolate. Cravings for certain foods may be due to the area you were brought up in... and your family traditions.

Many people were brought up with soda. Harvard public health in 2013 showed about 25,000 obesity related deaths in the US are linked to the large intake of soda. An average 20 oz bottle of soda will take miles of running or walking to burn off. In the production of Coca-Cola 300,000 tons of aluminum are used each year to make cans which is 17.4% of US aluminum production. What a statistic. That in itself isn't good for us humans or the environment but it shows Coca-Cola's size. Coca-Cola is also the largest buyer of sugar in the world. Then in addition to that some sodas used an ingredient, a retardant, called brominated vegetable oil (BVO) which has been banned in Europe and Japan...it was rated toxic yet it could be found in American soft drinks like Squirt, Sun drop, 7 up, Dr Pepper, Sunkist, orange Gatorade, orange Mountain Dew, Crush orange, crushed pineapple, Fanta, Fresca and possibly others. Daily calorie intake for children from soda is 11%. 63% of Americans report having at least one soda per day! A family of four that makes $29,000 per year takes 8.8% of their calories from soda... For incomes around $77,000 it's 4.4%. 93% of the world's population recognized Coca-Cola's logo and 2 billion servings are consumed each day ... .and that's just one manufacturer. Of the 33,000 items for sale on the supermarket Coke is the number one selling item. Sugar drinks can be cheaper than water. We consume more of them than water.

Individual health is not the only concern with this obesity epidemic. National Defense has been compromised. 70% of active duty service members are overweight. 77% of American youth between 17 and 24 cannot qualify for any branch of the service. Sugar doesn't only cause diabetes. Children's teeth are suffering. Oral health has been degrading since the sugar industry paid scientists in the 1960s to play down the link between sugar and heart disease and blame fat for the heart diseases increasing numbers. The use of sugar in foods exploded as sugar replaced fat. Candy in various forms will stick to teeth and get in all those crevices. Kids' teeth can decay to the roots in as little as 6 months. Children are having their teeth taken out in record numbers. Credit Suisse Bank has concluded that sugar increases type 2 diabetes, obesity, and metabolic syndrome (a cluster of conditions that occur together). Metabolic syndrome includes high blood pressure, high blood sugar, excess cholesterol and body fat all of which increases the chance of heart attack, stroke, diabetes and cancer. Research says if there is one thing you can do for your health it would be to stop eating sugar.

It is said that government intervention must occur for things to change. We don't give our kids tobacco to smoke, we don't give our kids alcohol to drink, but we give our kids soft drinks to drink? It's a public health hazard. We must remove sugar from the food. The cost to the healthcare system is tremendous. It's obvious when you are presented with the statistic that every six seconds someone dies from diabetes. Harvard health estimates by the end of the decade 49% of the US will be obese... that's half! It's our food. Some of our food is banned in China and the European Union. Many foods we eat in the US are on their "Do not eat" list. Whether it's the fat, or most especially trans fat, excessive sodium, preservatives, synthetic hormone dyes or flavorings, genetic engineering, the way it is formed, or additives the rest of the world questions US food. Ultra processed food makes up half of all calories in the US diet. All of this should question how much food we consume actually comes from the farm versus a lab-oriented facility... .and that's just the normal food we eat compared to the junk food that we have for snacks which is far worse. People have 2/3 of their stomach removed to prevent them from the prognosis of death.. 135,000 had that operation last year. We shouldn't have statistics like that.

With all this it is up to the individual to take steps to avoid these terrible health issues. The desire to do so isn't hard to instill in yourself or those you love... or anybody. Common sense should guide you to a healthier lifestyle. By controlling food consumption and exercising enough we can enjoy the benefits of bodily care physically, socially and mentally. Reverting to how our body is designed to work should be investigated and implemented by everyone. We can all do it. Many are in the areas that are food deserts….an area in which it is difficult to buy affordable or good quality fresh food. Then there are those who cannot cook or don't have a place to cook….. but as it has been said all things are possible.

Poison is defined as a substance that is capable of causing illness or death of a living organism when introduced or absorbed. That is what the majority of our diet is... poison. Just looking at the statistics at the Center for Disease Control it says that more than 90% of Americans will get too much salt... It will kill you.

Sitting in front of the post office, watching all the overweight people hobble across the street brings the epidemic closer to home. They don't look like they've had a lifetime of self-care. They waddle instead of walk. Self-indulgence, compulsive reactions and an undisciplined structure of life got them there.

4 billion gallons of ice cream is made each year worldwide …it is calculated that 23.2 quarts are consumed by each American. I eat almost none, so some are eating way more than that….but the question is …will you be giving it to those you love?